50 American Tea-Time Treats

By: Kelly Johnson

Table of Contents

- Scones
- Lemon bars
- Chocolate chip cookies
- Brownies
- Cornbread
- Pumpkin bread
- Banana bread
- Apple pie
- Cherry pie
- Pecan pie
- Oatmeal raisin cookies
- Snickerdoodles
- Whoopie pies
- Bundt cake
- Coffee cake
- Blueberry muffins
- Lemon poppy seed muffins
- Gingerbread cookies
- Shortbread cookies
- Cheesecake
- Rice Krispies treats
- Chocolate cake
- Carrot cake
- Red velvet cake
- Coconut macaroons
- Peanut butter cookies
- Hummingbird cake
- Key lime pie
- Pineapple upside-down cake
- Chocolate mousse
- Pudding cups
- Strawberry shortcake
- Almond cake
- Caramel cake
- Cinnamon rolls

- Biscotti
- Oatmeal cookies
- Tea breads
- Fig newtons
- Apple cider donuts
- Sweet potato pie
- Lemon meringue pie
- Churros
- Tiramisu
- Fruit tarts
- Jell-O parfaits
- Molasses cookies
- Hot milk cake
- Chocolate truffles
- Icebox cake

Scones

Ingredients:

- 2 cups (250g) all-purpose flour
- 1/4 cup (50g) granulated sugar
- 1 tbsp baking powder
- 1/2 tsp salt
- 1/2 cup (113g) unsalted butter, cold and cubed
- 1/2 cup (120ml) heavy cream (plus extra for brushing)
- 1 large egg
- 1 tsp vanilla extract

Instructions:

1. Preheat oven to 400°F (200°C) and line a baking sheet with parchment paper.
2. In a large bowl, whisk together flour, sugar, baking powder, and salt.
3. Cut cold butter into the flour mixture until it resembles coarse crumbs.
4. In a separate bowl, whisk together cream, egg, and vanilla.
5. Add wet ingredients to dry ingredients and mix until just combined.
6. Turn dough onto a floured surface, knead gently, then shape it into a 1-inch thick circle.
7. Cut into 8 wedges and place on a baking sheet. Brush with cream and bake for 15-18 minutes until golden brown.

Lemon Bars

Ingredients:

For the crust:

- 1 1/2 cups (190g) all-purpose flour
- 1/4 cup (50g) powdered sugar
- 1/2 cup (115g) unsalted butter, cold and cubed

For the filling:

- 1 1/2 cups (300g) granulated sugar
- 1 tbsp all-purpose flour
- 1/4 tsp baking powder
- 3 large eggs
- 1/2 cup (120ml) fresh lemon juice
- Zest of 1 lemon

Instructions:

1. Preheat oven to 350°F (180°C). Grease an 8x8-inch baking dish.
2. For the crust: Mix flour, powdered sugar, and butter, then press into the bottom of the baking dish.
3. Bake for 15-20 minutes until light golden.
4. For the filling: Whisk sugar, flour, baking powder, eggs, lemon juice, and zest.
5. Pour filling over baked crust and bake for 20-25 minutes until set.
6. Cool, then cut into squares and dust with powdered sugar.

Chocolate Chip Cookies

Ingredients:

- 2 1/4 cups (280g) all-purpose flour
- 1/2 tsp baking soda
- 1/2 tsp salt
- 3/4 cup (170g) unsalted butter, softened
- 1 cup (200g) granulated sugar
- 1/2 cup (100g) packed brown sugar
- 2 large eggs
- 2 tsp vanilla extract
- 2 cups (340g) chocolate chips

Instructions:

1. Preheat oven to 350°F (180°C) and line a baking sheet with parchment paper.
2. In a bowl, whisk together flour, baking soda, and salt.
3. Beat butter, granulated sugar, and brown sugar until fluffy. Add eggs and vanilla, then beat until combined.
4. Gradually add flour mixture and mix until combined. Stir in chocolate chips.
5. Drop spoonfuls of dough onto the baking sheet, spacing them apart.
6. Bake for 10-12 minutes until edges are golden.

Brownies

Ingredients:

- 1 cup (225g) unsalted butter
- 1 1/2 cups (300g) granulated sugar
- 1/2 cup (100g) brown sugar
- 1 tsp vanilla extract
- 4 large eggs
- 1 cup (125g) all-purpose flour
- 1/2 cup (45g) unsweetened cocoa powder
- 1/4 tsp salt

Instructions:

1. Preheat oven to 350°F (180°C) and grease a 9x9-inch baking pan.
2. Melt butter and stir in sugars and vanilla. Beat in eggs, one at a time.
3. Stir in flour, cocoa powder, and salt until combined.
4. Pour into the prepared pan and bake for 25-30 minutes until a toothpick comes out clean.
5. Cool before slicing into squares.

Cornbread

Ingredients:

- 1 cup (120g) cornmeal
- 1 cup (125g) all-purpose flour
- 1/4 cup (50g) sugar
- 1 tsp baking powder
- 1/2 tsp salt
- 1/4 cup (60g) unsalted butter, melted
- 1 cup (240ml) buttermilk
- 2 large eggs

Instructions:

1. Preheat oven to 375°F (190°C) and grease a 9x9-inch pan.
2. In a bowl, whisk together cornmeal, flour, sugar, baking powder, and salt.
3. In another bowl, whisk together melted butter, buttermilk, and eggs.
4. Add wet ingredients to dry and mix until combined.
5. Pour into the pan and bake for 20-25 minutes until golden.

Pumpkin Bread

Ingredients:

- 1 3/4 cups (220g) all-purpose flour
- 1 tsp baking soda
- 1/2 tsp salt
- 1 tsp ground cinnamon
- 1/2 tsp ground nutmeg
- 1/2 cup (100g) granulated sugar
- 1/2 cup (100g) brown sugar
- 1/2 cup (120ml) vegetable oil
- 2 large eggs
- 1 1/2 cups (360g) canned pumpkin

Instructions:

1. Preheat oven to 350°F (180°C) and grease a loaf pan.
2. In a bowl, whisk together flour, baking soda, salt, cinnamon, and nutmeg.
3. In another bowl, beat together sugars, oil, eggs, and pumpkin.
4. Gradually add the dry ingredients and mix until combined.
5. Pour batter into the pan and bake for 50-60 minutes until a toothpick comes out clean.

Banana Bread

Ingredients:

- 2-3 ripe bananas, mashed
- 1 1/2 cups (190g) all-purpose flour
- 1 tsp baking soda
- 1/4 tsp salt
- 1/2 cup (115g) unsalted butter, softened
- 1/2 cup (100g) granulated sugar
- 2 large eggs
- 1 tsp vanilla extract

Instructions:

1. Preheat oven to 350°F (180°C) and grease a loaf pan.
2. In a bowl, whisk together flour, baking soda, and salt.
3. In another bowl, beat butter, sugar, eggs, and mashed bananas.
4. Gradually add dry ingredients and mix until just combined.
5. Pour batter into the pan and bake for 60-65 minutes until golden and a toothpick comes out clean.

Apple Pie

Ingredients:

For the crust:

- 2 1/2 cups (310g) all-purpose flour
- 1 tsp salt
- 1 cup (230g) unsalted butter, cold and cubed
- 1/4 cup (60ml) cold water

For the filling:

- 6-8 medium apples, peeled, cored, and sliced
- 3/4 cup (150g) granulated sugar
- 1/4 cup (50g) brown sugar
- 1 tsp cinnamon
- 1 tbsp lemon juice

Instructions:

1. Preheat oven to 425°F (220°C).
2. For the crust: Mix flour and salt, then cut in butter until crumbly. Add cold water and form dough.
3. Roll out dough, place one layer in a pie dish, and fill with sliced apples, sugar, cinnamon, and lemon juice.
4. Roll out the second layer of dough and place over the filling. Cut slits for ventilation.
5. Bake for 45-50 minutes until golden and bubbly.

Cherry Pie

Ingredients:

For the crust:

- 2 1/2 cups (310g) all-purpose flour
- 1 tsp salt
- 1 cup (230g) unsalted butter, cold and cubed
- 1/4 cup (60ml) cold water

For the filling:

- 4 cups fresh or frozen cherries
- 3/4 cup (150g) granulated sugar
- 2 tbsp cornstarch
- 1 tbsp lemon juice

Instructions:

1. Preheat oven to 425°F (220°C).
2. For the crust: Mix flour and salt, then cut in butter until crumbly. Add cold water and form dough.
3. Roll out dough, place in a pie dish, and fill with cherries, sugar, cornstarch, and lemon juice.
4. Roll out the second layer of dough and place over the filling. Cut slits for ventilation.
5. Bake for 40-45 minutes until golden and bubbly.

Pecan Pie

Ingredients:

- 1 1/2 cups (150g) pecan halves
- 3/4 cup (150g) granulated sugar
- 1/4 cup (50g) brown sugar
- 1 cup (240ml) corn syrup
- 3 large eggs
- 1/4 cup (60g) unsalted butter, melted
- 1 tsp vanilla extract
- 1 tsp salt

Instructions:

1. Preheat oven to 350°F (180°C).
2. In a bowl, whisk together sugar, brown sugar, corn syrup, eggs, butter, vanilla, and salt.
3. Stir in pecans and pour mixture into an unbaked pie crust.
4. Bake for 45-50 minutes until the filling is set and golden.

Oatmeal Raisin Cookies

Ingredients:

- 1 cup (115g) rolled oats
- 3/4 cup (90g) all-purpose flour
- 1/2 tsp baking soda
- 1/2 tsp cinnamon
- 1/4 tsp salt
- 1/2 cup (115g) unsalted butter, softened
- 1/2 cup (100g) granulated sugar
- 1/2 cup (100g) brown sugar
- 1 large egg
- 1 tsp vanilla extract
- 1 cup (150g) raisins

Instructions:

1. Preheat oven to 350°F (180°C) and line a baking sheet with parchment paper.
2. In a bowl, whisk together oats, flour, baking soda, cinnamon, and salt.
3. Beat butter, sugar, and brown sugar until light and fluffy.
4. Add egg and vanilla, then mix in dry ingredients.
5. Stir in raisins.
6. Drop spoonfuls of dough onto the baking sheet and bake for 10-12 minutes until golden.

Snickerdoodles

Ingredients:

- 2 3/4 cups (345g) all-purpose flour
- 1 1/2 tsp cream of tartar
- 1 tsp baking soda
- 1/2 tsp salt
- 1 cup (225g) unsalted butter, softened
- 1 1/4 cups (250g) granulated sugar
- 2 large eggs
- 1 tsp vanilla extract
- 1/4 cup (50g) granulated sugar (for rolling)
- 2 tsp ground cinnamon (for rolling)

Instructions:

1. Preheat oven to 350°F (180°C) and line a baking sheet with parchment paper.
2. In a bowl, whisk together flour, cream of tartar, baking soda, and salt.
3. Beat butter and sugar until light and fluffy.
4. Add eggs and vanilla, then mix in dry ingredients.
5. Roll dough into 1-inch balls and roll in cinnamon-sugar mixture.
6. Bake for 8-10 minutes until lightly golden.

Whoopie Pies

Ingredients:

For the cakes:

- 2 1/2 cups (315g) all-purpose flour
- 1 tsp baking powder
- 1/2 tsp baking soda
- 1/2 cup (50g) unsweetened cocoa powder
- 1/2 tsp salt
- 1 cup (225g) unsalted butter, softened
- 1 1/4 cups (250g) granulated sugar
- 2 large eggs
- 1 tsp vanilla extract
- 1 cup (240ml) buttermilk

For the filling:

- 1/2 cup (115g) unsalted butter, softened
- 1 1/2 cups (180g) powdered sugar
- 1 cup (240g) marshmallow fluff
- 1 tsp vanilla extract

Instructions:

1. Preheat oven to 350°F (180°C) and line a baking sheet with parchment paper.
2. In a bowl, whisk together flour, cocoa powder, baking powder, baking soda, and salt.
3. Beat butter and sugar until light and fluffy.
4. Add eggs and vanilla, then alternate adding dry ingredients and buttermilk.
5. Drop tablespoon-sized scoops of dough onto the baking sheet.
6. Bake for 8-10 minutes, let cool.
7. For the filling, beat butter, powdered sugar, marshmallow fluff, and vanilla.
8. Spread filling between two cakes to form pies.

Bundt Cake

Ingredients:

- 2 1/2 cups (310g) all-purpose flour
- 1 tsp baking powder
- 1/2 tsp baking soda
- 1/2 tsp salt
- 1 cup (225g) unsalted butter, softened
- 1 1/2 cups (300g) granulated sugar
- 4 large eggs
- 1 1/2 tsp vanilla extract
- 1 cup (240ml) sour cream

Instructions:

1. Preheat oven to 350°F (180°C) and grease a bundt pan.
2. In a bowl, whisk together flour, baking powder, baking soda, and salt.
3. Beat butter and sugar until fluffy.
4. Add eggs one at a time, then mix in vanilla.
5. Gradually add dry ingredients and sour cream, mixing until smooth.
6. Pour batter into bundt pan and bake for 45-50 minutes until a toothpick comes out clean.

Coffee Cake

Ingredients:

For the cake:

- 2 1/2 cups (310g) all-purpose flour
- 1 tsp baking powder
- 1/2 tsp baking soda
- 1/4 tsp salt
- 1/2 cup (115g) unsalted butter, softened
- 1 cup (200g) granulated sugar
- 2 large eggs
- 1 tsp vanilla extract
- 1 cup (240ml) sour cream

For the topping:

- 1/2 cup (100g) brown sugar
- 1/4 cup (30g) all-purpose flour
- 1 tsp ground cinnamon
- 2 tbsp unsalted butter, softened

Instructions:

1. Preheat oven to 350°F (180°C) and grease a 9-inch cake pan.
2. In a bowl, whisk together flour, baking powder, baking soda, and salt.
3. Beat butter and sugar until light and fluffy.
4. Add eggs and vanilla, then stir in sour cream.
5. Gradually add dry ingredients and mix until combined.
6. For the topping, mix brown sugar, flour, cinnamon, and butter.
7. Pour batter into the pan, sprinkle topping on top, and bake for 30-35 minutes.

Blueberry Muffins

Ingredients:

- 2 cups (250g) all-purpose flour
- 1/2 cup (100g) granulated sugar
- 1 tsp baking powder
- 1/2 tsp baking soda
- 1/4 tsp salt
- 1/2 cup (120ml) milk
- 1/4 cup (60g) unsalted butter, melted
- 2 large eggs
- 1 tsp vanilla extract
- 1 1/2 cups (200g) fresh blueberries

Instructions:

1. Preheat oven to 375°F (190°C) and line a muffin tin with paper liners.
2. In a bowl, whisk together flour, sugar, baking powder, baking soda, and salt.
3. In a separate bowl, whisk together milk, butter, eggs, and vanilla.
4. Gradually add wet ingredients to dry ingredients, then fold in blueberries.
5. Spoon batter into muffin tin and bake for 20-25 minutes until golden.

Lemon Poppy Seed Muffins

Ingredients:

- 2 cups (250g) all-purpose flour
- 1 cup (200g) granulated sugar
- 1 tsp baking powder
- 1/2 tsp baking soda
- 1/4 tsp salt
- 2 tbsp poppy seeds
- 1/2 cup (120ml) milk
- 1/4 cup (60g) unsalted butter, melted
- 2 large eggs
- Zest and juice of 1 lemon

Instructions:

1. Preheat oven to 375°F (190°C) and line a muffin tin with paper liners.
2. In a bowl, whisk together flour, sugar, baking powder, baking soda, salt, and poppy seeds.
3. In a separate bowl, whisk together milk, butter, eggs, and lemon zest and juice.
4. Add wet ingredients to dry ingredients and mix until combined.
5. Spoon batter into muffin tin and bake for 18-20 minutes until golden.

Gingerbread Cookies

Ingredients:

- 3 1/4 cups (400g) all-purpose flour
- 1 tsp ground ginger
- 1 tsp cinnamon
- 1/4 tsp ground cloves
- 1/2 tsp baking soda
- 1/4 tsp salt
- 1/2 cup (115g) unsalted butter, softened
- 1/2 cup (100g) brown sugar
- 1 large egg
- 1/2 cup (120g) molasses

Instructions:

1. Preheat oven to 350°F (180°C) and line a baking sheet with parchment paper.
2. In a bowl, whisk together flour, spices, baking soda, and salt.
3. Beat butter and brown sugar until fluffy. Add egg and molasses and mix well.
4. Gradually add dry ingredients and mix until smooth.
5. Roll out dough and cut into shapes, then bake for 8-10 minutes.

Shortbread Cookies

Ingredients:

- 2 cups (250g) all-purpose flour
- 1/2 cup (100g) granulated sugar
- 1 cup (225g) unsalted butter, softened
- 1/4 tsp salt

Instructions:

1. Preheat oven to 325°F (160°C) and line a baking sheet with parchment paper.
2. Beat butter, sugar, and salt until smooth. Gradually add flour and mix until a dough forms.
3. Roll dough into a log, slice into rounds, and place on the baking sheet.
4. Bake for 15-18 minutes until lightly golden.

Cheesecake

Ingredients:

For the crust:

- 1 1/2 cups (180g) graham cracker crumbs
- 1/4 cup (50g) granulated sugar
- 1/2 cup (115g) unsalted butter, melted

For the filling:

- 4 packages (900g) cream cheese, softened
- 1 cup (200g) granulated sugar
- 1 tsp vanilla extract
- 4 large eggs
- 1 cup (240ml) sour cream

Instructions:

1. Preheat oven to 325°F (160°C) and grease a 9-inch springform pan.
2. Mix graham cracker crumbs, sugar, and melted butter, then press into the bottom of the pan.
3. Beat cream cheese, sugar, and vanilla until smooth. Add eggs one at a time.
4. Pour filling over the crust and bake for 55-60 minutes.
5. Cool and refrigerate for at least 4 hours before serving.

Rice Krispies Treats

Ingredients:

- 6 cups (180g) Rice Krispies cereal
- 3 tbsp unsalted butter
- 1 package (10 oz) marshmallows

Instructions:

1. Melt butter in a large pot over medium heat.
2. Add marshmallows and stir until melted.
3. Remove from heat and stir in Rice Krispies until well coated.
4. Press mixture into a greased 9x9-inch pan and let cool.
5. Cut into squares and enjoy!

Chocolate Cake

Ingredients:

- 1 3/4 cups (220g) all-purpose flour
- 1 1/2 cups (300g) granulated sugar
- 3/4 cup (75g) unsweetened cocoa powder
- 1 1/2 tsp baking powder
- 1 1/2 tsp baking soda
- 1 tsp salt
- 2 large eggs
- 1 cup (240ml) milk
- 1/2 cup (120ml) vegetable oil
- 2 tsp vanilla extract
- 1 cup (240ml) boiling water

Instructions:

1. Preheat oven to 350°F (175°C) and grease two 9-inch round cake pans.
2. In a large bowl, whisk together flour, sugar, cocoa, baking powder, baking soda, and salt.
3. Add eggs, milk, oil, and vanilla, and mix until smooth.
4. Stir in boiling water until the batter is thin.
5. Pour batter evenly into prepared pans and bake for 30-35 minutes, or until a toothpick comes out clean.
6. Let cakes cool in pans for 10 minutes, then transfer to wire racks to cool completely.

Carrot Cake

Ingredients:

- 2 cups (250g) all-purpose flour
- 1 1/2 tsp baking powder
- 1 1/2 tsp baking soda
- 1/2 tsp salt
- 1 tsp ground cinnamon
- 1/2 tsp ground nutmeg
- 4 large eggs
- 1 1/2 cups (300g) granulated sugar
- 1/2 cup (120ml) vegetable oil
- 2 cups (250g) grated carrots
- 1 cup (100g) chopped walnuts (optional)

For the frosting:

- 8 oz (225g) cream cheese, softened
- 1/4 cup (60g) unsalted butter, softened
- 2 cups (250g) powdered sugar
- 1 tsp vanilla extract

Instructions:

1. Preheat oven to 350°F (175°C) and grease and flour two 9-inch round cake pans.
2. In a bowl, whisk together flour, baking powder, baking soda, salt, cinnamon, and nutmeg.
3. In another bowl, beat eggs and sugar until fluffy. Add oil, then mix in dry ingredients.
4. Stir in grated carrots and walnuts (if using).
5. Pour batter into pans and bake for 30-35 minutes. Cool in pans for 10 minutes, then transfer to wire racks.
6. For frosting, beat cream cheese and butter until smooth. Gradually add powdered sugar and vanilla, then frost cooled cakes.

Red Velvet Cake

Ingredients:

- 2 1/2 cups (315g) all-purpose flour
- 1 1/2 cups (300g) granulated sugar
- 1 tsp baking powder
- 1 tsp baking soda
- 1/2 tsp salt
- 1 tbsp cocoa powder
- 1 1/2 cups (360ml) buttermilk
- 1/2 cup (120ml) vegetable oil
- 2 large eggs
- 1 tsp vanilla extract
- 2 tbsp red food coloring

For the frosting:

- 8 oz (225g) cream cheese, softened
- 1/2 cup (115g) unsalted butter, softened
- 4 cups (500g) powdered sugar
- 1 tsp vanilla extract

Instructions:

1. Preheat oven to 350°F (175°C) and grease two 9-inch round cake pans.
2. In a bowl, whisk together flour, sugar, baking powder, baking soda, salt, and cocoa powder.
3. In another bowl, mix buttermilk, oil, eggs, vanilla, and food coloring.
4. Add wet ingredients to dry ingredients and mix until smooth.
5. Pour batter into pans and bake for 25-30 minutes. Cool in pans for 10 minutes, then transfer to wire racks.
6. For frosting, beat cream cheese and butter until smooth, then gradually add powdered sugar and vanilla. Frost cooled cakes.

Coconut Macaroons

Ingredients:

- 2 1/2 cups (200g) shredded coconut
- 2/3 cup (130g) granulated sugar
- 1/4 tsp salt
- 2 large egg whites
- 1 tsp vanilla extract

Instructions:

1. Preheat oven to 325°F (160°C) and line a baking sheet with parchment paper.
2. In a bowl, mix coconut, sugar, and salt.
3. Beat egg whites until stiff peaks form, then fold into coconut mixture.
4. Spoon batter into small mounds on the baking sheet.
5. Bake for 15-20 minutes until golden brown. Let cool before serving.

Peanut Butter Cookies

Ingredients:

- 1 cup (250g) peanut butter
- 1 cup (200g) granulated sugar
- 1 egg
- 1 tsp vanilla extract
- 1/2 tsp baking soda

Instructions:

1. Preheat oven to 350°F (175°C) and line a baking sheet with parchment paper.
2. Mix peanut butter, sugar, egg, vanilla, and baking soda until smooth.
3. Roll dough into balls and place on the baking sheet. Flatten with a fork.
4. Bake for 8-10 minutes until golden. Let cool on the baking sheet.

Hummingbird Cake

Ingredients:

- 3 cups (375g) all-purpose flour
- 1 1/2 tsp baking soda
- 1 tsp ground cinnamon
- 1/2 tsp salt
- 2 cups (400g) granulated sugar
- 3 large eggs
- 1 1/2 cups (360ml) vegetable oil
- 1 tsp vanilla extract
- 1 1/2 cups (375g) mashed ripe bananas
- 1 cup (240g) crushed pineapple, drained
- 1 cup (100g) chopped pecans

For the frosting:

- 8 oz (225g) cream cheese, softened
- 1/4 cup (60g) unsalted butter, softened
- 4 cups (500g) powdered sugar
- 1 tsp vanilla extract

Instructions:

1. Preheat oven to 350°F (175°C) and grease and flour two 9-inch round cake pans.
2. In a bowl, whisk together flour, baking soda, cinnamon, and salt.
3. Beat sugar, eggs, and oil until fluffy. Add vanilla, bananas, pineapple, and chopped pecans.
4. Gradually add dry ingredients and mix until smooth.
5. Pour batter into pans and bake for 30-35 minutes. Cool in pans for 10 minutes, then transfer to wire racks.
6. For frosting, beat cream cheese and butter until smooth. Gradually add powdered sugar and vanilla. Frost cooled cakes.

Key Lime Pie

Ingredients:

For the crust:

- 1 1/2 cups (180g) graham cracker crumbs
- 1/4 cup (50g) granulated sugar
- 1/2 cup (115g) unsalted butter, melted

For the filling:

- 1 can (14 oz/400g) sweetened condensed milk
- 1/2 cup (120ml) fresh lime juice
- Zest of 2 limes
- 3 large egg yolks

Instructions:

1. Preheat oven to 350°F (175°C).
2. For the crust: Mix graham cracker crumbs, sugar, and butter, then press into the bottom of a 9-inch pie pan.
3. Bake for 10-12 minutes until golden.
4. For the filling: Mix sweetened condensed milk, lime juice, lime zest, and egg yolks until smooth.
5. Pour into crust and bake for 15-20 minutes until set. Let cool, then refrigerate for 2-3 hours.

Pineapple Upside-Down Cake

Ingredients:

For the topping:

- 1/4 cup (60g) unsalted butter
- 1/2 cup (100g) brown sugar
- 8-10 pineapple rings, drained
- Maraschino cherries

For the cake:

- 1 1/2 cups (190g) all-purpose flour
- 1 1/2 tsp baking powder
- 1/4 tsp salt
- 1/2 cup (115g) unsalted butter, softened
- 1 cup (200g) granulated sugar
- 2 large eggs
- 1 tsp vanilla extract
- 1/2 cup (120ml) milk

Instructions:

1. Preheat oven to 350°F (175°C) and grease a 9-inch round cake pan.
2. For the topping: Melt butter and brown sugar in the cake pan, then arrange pineapple rings and cherries in the bottom.
3. For the cake: In a bowl, mix flour, baking powder, and salt.
4. Beat butter and sugar until fluffy, then add eggs and vanilla. Gradually add dry ingredients and milk.
5. Pour batter over pineapple and bake for 30-35 minutes until golden.
6. Let cool for 10 minutes, then invert onto a plate.

Chocolate Mousse

Ingredients:

- 6 oz (170g) dark chocolate, chopped
- 1 cup (240ml) heavy cream
- 2 tbsp sugar
- 2 large egg whites
- 2 tbsp granulated sugar

Instructions:

1. Melt chocolate in a heatproof bowl over simmering water or in the microwave.
2. In a separate bowl, whip heavy cream with sugar until stiff peaks form.
3. In another bowl, beat egg whites with sugar until stiff peaks form.
4. Gently fold the melted chocolate into whipped cream, then fold in egg whites.
5. Spoon into serving glasses and refrigerate for at least 2 hours before serving.

Pudding Cups

Ingredients:

- 2 cups (480ml) whole milk
- 1/2 cup (100g) sugar
- 3 tbsp cornstarch
- 1/4 tsp salt
- 2 large egg yolks
- 1 tsp vanilla extract

Instructions:

1. In a saucepan, combine milk, sugar, cornstarch, and salt. Cook over medium heat, whisking constantly until thickened.
2. In a bowl, whisk egg yolks. Gradually add a little hot milk mixture to temper the eggs.
3. Slowly pour egg mixture back into the saucepan and cook for 2 minutes.
4. Stir in vanilla and pour into cups. Refrigerate for 2-3 hours before serving.

Strawberry Shortcake

Ingredients:

For the shortcakes:

- 2 cups (250g) all-purpose flour
- 1/4 cup (50g) sugar
- 1 tbsp baking powder
- 1/4 tsp salt
- 1/2 cup (115g) unsalted butter, cold and cubed
- 1/2 cup (120ml) heavy cream

For the filling:

- 2 cups (300g) fresh strawberries, sliced
- 1/4 cup (50g) sugar
- 1 cup (240ml) heavy cream

Instructions:

1. Preheat oven to 400°F (200°C) and line a baking sheet with parchment paper.
2. For the shortcakes: Mix flour, sugar, baking powder, and salt. Cut in cold butter until crumbly. Stir in cream.
3. Drop spoonfuls of dough onto the baking sheet and bake for 12-15 minutes until golden.
4. For the filling: Toss strawberries with sugar and let sit for 10 minutes.
5. Whip heavy cream to stiff peaks.
6. Assemble by splitting shortcakes, layering with whipped cream and strawberries, and serving.

Almond Cake

Ingredients:

- 1 1/2 cups (190g) all-purpose flour
- 1 1/2 tsp baking powder
- 1/4 tsp salt
- 1 cup (200g) granulated sugar
- 1/2 cup (115g) unsalted butter, softened
- 2 large eggs
- 1 tsp vanilla extract
- 1 tsp almond extract
- 1/2 cup (120ml) milk
- 1/2 cup (50g) sliced almonds

Instructions:

1. Preheat oven to 350°F (175°C) and grease and flour a 9-inch round cake pan.
2. In a bowl, whisk together flour, baking powder, and salt.
3. Beat butter and sugar until light and fluffy. Add eggs, one at a time, followed by vanilla and almond extract.
4. Gradually add flour mixture, alternating with milk. Stir in sliced almonds.
5. Pour batter into the prepared pan and bake for 25-30 minutes, or until a toothpick comes out clean.
6. Let cool in the pan for 10 minutes, then transfer to a wire rack to cool completely.

Caramel Cake

Ingredients:

For the cake:

- 2 1/2 cups (315g) all-purpose flour
- 1 1/2 tsp baking powder
- 1/2 tsp baking soda
- 1/2 tsp salt
- 1 cup (240ml) buttermilk
- 1 cup (230g) granulated sugar
- 1/2 cup (115g) unsalted butter, softened
- 2 large eggs
- 1 tsp vanilla extract

For the caramel frosting:

- 1/2 cup (115g) unsalted butter
- 1 cup (200g) brown sugar
- 1/4 cup (60ml) milk
- 1 1/2 cups (190g) powdered sugar

Instructions:

1. Preheat oven to 350°F (175°C) and grease and flour two 9-inch round cake pans.
2. In a bowl, whisk together flour, baking powder, baking soda, and salt.
3. In another bowl, beat sugar and butter until fluffy. Add eggs and vanilla.
4. Gradually add dry ingredients alternating with buttermilk.
5. Pour batter into pans and bake for 30-35 minutes. Let cool.
6. For frosting: Melt butter in a saucepan. Stir in brown sugar and milk, and bring to a boil. Remove from heat and add powdered sugar.
7. Frost cooled cakes with the caramel frosting.

Cinnamon Rolls

Ingredients:

For the dough:

- 3 1/2 cups (440g) all-purpose flour
- 1/4 cup (50g) granulated sugar
- 1 tbsp instant yeast
- 1/2 tsp salt
- 1 cup (240ml) warm milk
- 1/4 cup (60g) unsalted butter, melted
- 2 large eggs

For the filling:

- 1/2 cup (115g) unsalted butter, softened
- 1 cup (200g) brown sugar
- 2 tbsp ground cinnamon

For the icing:

- 1 cup (120g) powdered sugar
- 2 tbsp milk
- 1/2 tsp vanilla extract

Instructions:

1. In a large bowl, combine flour, sugar, yeast, and salt. Add warm milk, butter, and eggs, and mix until a dough forms.
2. Knead dough for 5-7 minutes, then cover and let rise for 1-2 hours.
3. Preheat oven to 350°F (175°C) and grease a baking dish.
4. Roll dough into a rectangle, spread with softened butter, and sprinkle with brown sugar and cinnamon.
5. Roll up dough tightly, slice into rolls, and place in the prepared dish.
6. Bake for 25-30 minutes, or until golden.
7. Mix powdered sugar, milk, and vanilla to make the icing. Drizzle over warm cinnamon rolls.

Biscotti

Ingredients:

- 2 cups (250g) all-purpose flour
- 1 tsp baking powder
- 1/4 tsp salt
- 3/4 cup (150g) granulated sugar
- 3 large eggs
- 1 tsp vanilla extract
- 1 cup (100g) almonds, chopped (optional)

Instructions:

1. Preheat oven to 350°F (175°C) and line a baking sheet with parchment paper.
2. In a bowl, whisk together flour, baking powder, and salt.
3. Beat eggs and sugar until light, then mix in vanilla.
4. Gradually add dry ingredients, and fold in chopped almonds.
5. Divide dough in half, form into two logs, and bake for 25-30 minutes.
6. Slice logs into 1-inch pieces and bake for an additional 10 minutes on each side until crisp.

Oatmeal Cookies

Ingredients:

- 1 cup (115g) rolled oats
- 1 cup (120g) all-purpose flour
- 1/2 tsp baking soda
- 1/2 tsp ground cinnamon
- 1/4 tsp salt
- 1/2 cup (115g) unsalted butter, softened
- 1/2 cup (100g) brown sugar
- 1/4 cup (50g) granulated sugar
- 1 large egg
- 1 tsp vanilla extract
- 1/2 cup (80g) raisins (optional)

Instructions:

1. Preheat oven to 350°F (175°C) and line a baking sheet with parchment paper.
2. In a bowl, mix oats, flour, baking soda, cinnamon, and salt.
3. Beat butter and sugars until creamy, then add egg and vanilla.
4. Gradually add dry ingredients and stir in raisins.
5. Drop spoonfuls of dough onto the baking sheet and bake for 10-12 minutes, until golden.

Tea Breads

Ingredients:

- 2 cups (250g) all-purpose flour
- 1 tbsp baking powder
- 1/2 tsp salt
- 1 cup (240ml) milk
- 1/2 cup (115g) unsalted butter, melted
- 1 large egg
- 1 cup (150g) dried fruit (raisins, currants, etc.)

Instructions:

1. Preheat oven to 350°F (175°C) and grease a loaf pan.
2. In a bowl, combine flour, baking powder, and salt.
3. In another bowl, mix milk, butter, and egg, then fold into the dry ingredients.
4. Stir in dried fruit.
5. Pour batter into the pan and bake for 45-50 minutes, or until a toothpick comes out clean.

Fig Newtons

Ingredients:

For the dough:

- 2 cups (250g) all-purpose flour
- 1/2 tsp baking soda
- 1/2 tsp salt
- 1/2 cup (115g) unsalted butter, softened
- 3/4 cup (150g) brown sugar
- 1 large egg
- 1 tsp vanilla extract

For the filling:

- 1 cup (150g) dried figs, chopped
- 1/4 cup (60ml) water
- 1 tbsp lemon juice
- 1/4 tsp ground cinnamon

Instructions:

1. Preheat oven to 350°F (175°C) and line a baking sheet with parchment paper.
2. Mix flour, baking soda, and salt in a bowl. Beat butter and sugar, then add egg and vanilla. Gradually mix in dry ingredients.
3. For the filling: In a saucepan, simmer figs, water, lemon juice, and cinnamon for 10-15 minutes. Blend into a paste.
4. Roll out dough and spread with fig filling. Roll up, slice into bars, and bake for 12-15 minutes.

Apple Cider Donuts

Ingredients:

- 2 cups (250g) all-purpose flour
- 1 tsp baking powder
- 1/2 tsp baking soda
- 1 tsp ground cinnamon
- 1/4 tsp ground nutmeg
- 1/2 tsp salt
- 1/2 cup (115g) unsalted butter, softened
- 3/4 cup (150g) granulated sugar
- 2 large eggs
- 1/2 cup (120ml) apple cider
- 1 tsp vanilla extract

Instructions:

1. Preheat oven to 350°F (175°C) and grease a donut pan.
2. Mix flour, baking powder, baking soda, cinnamon, nutmeg, and salt.
3. Beat butter and sugar until fluffy, then add eggs, apple cider, and vanilla. Gradually add dry ingredients.
4. Spoon batter into the donut pan and bake for 10-12 minutes.
5. Let cool, then dust with cinnamon sugar.

Sweet Potato Pie

Ingredients:

- 1 1/2 cups (360g) mashed sweet potatoes
- 1 cup (200g) granulated sugar
- 1/2 tsp ground cinnamon
- 1/4 tsp ground nutmeg
- 1/4 tsp salt
- 2 large eggs
- 1/2 cup (120ml) evaporated milk
- 1/2 tsp vanilla extract
- 1 pie crust

Instructions:

1. Preheat oven to 350°F (175°C) and line a pie pan with the pie crust.
2. Mix mashed sweet potatoes, sugar, cinnamon, nutmeg, and salt.
3. Beat in eggs, evaporated milk, and vanilla until smooth.
4. Pour mixture into the pie crust and bake for 45-50 minutes until set.

Lemon Meringue Pie

Ingredients:

For the filling:

- 1 cup (200g) granulated sugar
- 2 tbsp cornstarch
- 1/4 tsp salt
- 1 1/2 cups (360ml) water
- 3 large egg yolks
- 1/2 cup (120ml) fresh lemon juice
- 1 tbsp lemon zest
- 2 tbsp unsalted butter

For the meringue:

- 3 large egg whites
- 1/4 tsp cream of tartar
- 1/4 cup (50g) granulated sugar

Instructions:

1. Preheat oven to 350°F (175°C).
2. For the filling: Mix sugar, cornstarch, and salt in a saucepan. Gradually add water, and cook over medium heat until thickened.
3. Beat egg yolks, then temper with hot mixture. Return to the pan, stir in lemon juice, zest, and butter.
4. Pour filling into the pie crust and let cool.
5. For the meringue: Beat egg whites and cream of tartar until stiff peaks form. Gradually add sugar.
6. Spread meringue over the pie and bake for 10-12 minutes until golden.

Churros

Ingredients:

- 1 cup (240ml) water
- 2 tbsp granulated sugar
- 1/4 tsp salt
- 2 tbsp unsalted butter
- 1 cup (120g) all-purpose flour
- 2 large eggs
- Vegetable oil, for frying
- 1/2 cup (100g) granulated sugar
- 1 tsp ground cinnamon

Instructions:

1. In a saucepan, heat water, sugar, salt, and butter until boiling.
2. Remove from heat and stir in flour until smooth.
3. Beat in eggs until dough is thick.
4. Heat oil in a deep pan to 375°F (190°C).
5. Spoon dough into a piping bag with a star tip. Pipe dough into the hot oil, frying until golden brown.
6. Drain on paper towels, then roll in sugar and cinnamon.

Tiramisu

Ingredients:

- 1 1/2 cups (360ml) strong brewed coffee, cooled
- 1/4 cup (60ml) coffee liqueur (optional)
- 1 package (7 oz) ladyfinger cookies
- 1 1/2 cups (360ml) heavy cream
- 1/2 cup (100g) granulated sugar
- 1 tsp vanilla extract
- 1 package (8 oz) mascarpone cheese, softened
- 2 tbsp cocoa powder (for dusting)

Instructions:

1. In a shallow dish, combine coffee and coffee liqueur (if using). Set aside.
2. Whip heavy cream, sugar, and vanilla extract until stiff peaks form.
3. Gently fold mascarpone cheese into the whipped cream mixture.
4. Dip each ladyfinger into the coffee mixture for 1-2 seconds, then layer them in the bottom of a dish.
5. Spread half of the mascarpone mixture over the ladyfingers. Repeat with another layer of soaked ladyfingers and the remaining mascarpone mixture.
6. Refrigerate for at least 4 hours or overnight. Dust with cocoa powder before serving.

Fruit Tarts

Ingredients:

For the crust:

- 1 1/4 cups (160g) all-purpose flour
- 1/4 cup (50g) sugar
- 1/2 cup (115g) unsalted butter, cold and cubed
- 1 egg yolk
- 1-2 tbsp cold water

For the filling:

- 1 1/2 cups (360ml) heavy cream
- 1/2 cup (100g) sugar
- 1 tsp vanilla extract
- 1 tbsp cornstarch

For the topping:

- Assorted fresh fruit (berries, kiwi, etc.)
- 2 tbsp apricot jam (optional, for glazing)

Instructions:

1. Preheat oven to 350°F (175°C).
2. For the crust: Mix flour, sugar, and butter until it forms a crumbly mixture. Add egg yolk and cold water, then form into a dough. Roll out and fit into tart pans.
3. Bake for 12-15 minutes until golden. Let cool.
4. For the filling: Whisk together cream, sugar, vanilla, and cornstarch. Heat over medium heat until thickened.
5. Fill cooled tart shells with the cream mixture and arrange fresh fruit on top.
6. Optionally, heat apricot jam and brush over the fruit for a glossy finish.

Jell-O Parfaits

Ingredients:

- 1 box (3 oz) flavored Jell-O (any flavor)
- 1 cup (240ml) boiling water
- 1 cup (240ml) cold water
- 1 cup (240ml) whipped cream
- 1/4 cup (50g) granulated sugar

Instructions:

1. Dissolve the Jell-O in boiling water, then add cold water and stir well.
2. Pour Jell-O into serving cups and refrigerate until firm, about 2-3 hours.
3. Whip cream with sugar until stiff peaks form.
4. Once Jell-O is set, top with whipped cream and refrigerate until ready to serve.

Molasses Cookies

Ingredients:

- 2 1/4 cups (280g) all-purpose flour
- 1 tsp baking soda
- 1 1/2 tsp ground ginger
- 1 tsp ground cinnamon
- 1/4 tsp ground cloves
- 1/2 tsp salt
- 3/4 cup (170g) unsalted butter, softened
- 1 cup (200g) brown sugar
- 1/4 cup (60ml) molasses
- 1 large egg
- Granulated sugar (for rolling)

Instructions:

1. Preheat oven to 350°F (175°C) and line a baking sheet with parchment paper.
2. In a bowl, whisk together flour, baking soda, ginger, cinnamon, cloves, and salt.
3. Beat butter and brown sugar until fluffy. Add molasses, egg, and mix until combined.
4. Gradually add dry ingredients and mix until smooth.
5. Roll dough into 1-inch balls and roll in granulated sugar.
6. Place on the baking sheet and bake for 10-12 minutes until lightly golden.

Hot Milk Cake

Ingredients:

- 1 1/2 cups (190g) all-purpose flour
- 1 1/2 tsp baking powder
- 1/4 tsp salt
- 1/2 cup (120ml) milk
- 1/2 cup (115g) unsalted butter
- 1 tsp vanilla extract
- 1 cup (200g) granulated sugar
- 2 large eggs

Instructions:

1. Preheat oven to 350°F (175°C) and grease a 9-inch cake pan.
2. In a bowl, whisk together flour, baking powder, and salt.
3. In a saucepan, heat milk and butter over medium heat until butter is melted.
4. Beat eggs and sugar until fluffy, then gradually add the dry ingredients.
5. Stir in the warm milk and vanilla extract.
6. Pour batter into the cake pan and bake for 25-30 minutes until a toothpick comes out clean.

Chocolate Truffles

Ingredients:

- 8 oz (225g) semisweet or bittersweet chocolate, chopped
- 1/2 cup (120ml) heavy cream
- 1 tsp vanilla extract
- Cocoa powder, chopped nuts, or melted chocolate (for coating)

Instructions:

1. Place chopped chocolate in a heatproof bowl.
2. Heat cream in a saucepan until it just begins to simmer.
3. Pour the hot cream over the chocolate and let sit for 1-2 minutes, then stir until smooth.
4. Stir in vanilla extract and let the mixture cool to room temperature.
5. Refrigerate for 1-2 hours until firm.
6. Roll chilled ganache into small balls and coat with cocoa powder, chopped nuts, or melted chocolate.

Icebox Cake

Ingredients:

- 2 cups (480ml) heavy cream
- 1/4 cup (50g) granulated sugar
- 1 tsp vanilla extract
- 1 package (14 oz) graham crackers
- 1 cup (240g) chocolate pudding or custard (optional, for layers)

Instructions:

1. In a bowl, beat heavy cream, sugar, and vanilla until stiff peaks form.
2. On a serving dish, lay down a layer of graham crackers.
3. Spread a layer of whipped cream over the crackers. Repeat layers, alternating crackers and whipped cream, finishing with whipped cream on top.
4. Refrigerate for at least 4 hours or overnight to let the cake set and the crackers soften.
5. Optionally, top with chocolate pudding or custard and garnish with shaved chocolate or fruit before serving.